EASY FINGERPICKING GUITAR

by Andrew DuBrock

T0079538

PLAYBACK+
Speed • Pitch • Balance • Loop

To access audio visit:
www.halleonard.com/mylibrary

Enter Code
2049-9997-5990-5125

ISBN 978-1-61780-685-8

HAL•LEONARD®
7777 W. BLUEMOUND RD. P.O. BOX 13819 MILWAUKEE, WI 53213

In Australia Contact:
Hal Leonard Australia Pty. Ltd.
4 Lentara Court
Cheltenham, Victoria, 3192 Australia
Email: ausadmin@halleonard.com.au

Visit Hal Leonard Online at
www.halleonard.com

TABLE OF CONTENTS

ABOUT THE AUTHOR

Andrew DuBrock is an independent music consultant who lives in Portland, Oregon. He has worked as an editor, transcriber, engraver, and author for Hal Leonard, and served as Music Editor for *Acoustic Guitar, Strings,* and *Play Guitar!* magazines for seven years. A sampling of his instructional works include *Total Acoustic Guitar, Lennon and McCartney for Acoustic Guitar* (DVD), and *Rock/ Pop Guitar Songs for Dummies.* His independent acoustic pop/rock CD, *DuBrock,* can be found at *dubrock.net* and *cdbaby.com.*

To see more books and articles by Andrew DuBrock, or if you have comments or questions about this book, visit *andrewdubrock.com.*

INTRODUCTION

Whether you're completely new to guitar, you've strummed chords before but always wanted to fingerpick, or you've tried fingerpicking in the past but could never get the hang of it, this book is for you! The progressive approach in this book is designed to guide you through the basics of fingerpicking so that you can play many songs with multiple picking patterns—and even create countless patterns of your own! You *can* fingerpick the guitar!

GUITARS AND FINGERPICKS

You can fingerpick on most any guitar. Classical (and some "folk") acoustic guitars use nylon strings, which are easy on the fingers, and most people fingerpick these guitars. Steel-string guitars are more common with the pop, rock, bluegrass, celtic, and modern folk communities, and many players fingerpick these guitars, as well. The audio portion of this book was recorded with a steel-string guitar, by far the most popular type of acoustic guitar today. But, any guitar you choose to play will work fine for fingerpicking—even electric guitars!

Many players fingerpick with their bare fingers, and some grow out their nails to provide a brighter attack when plucking the strings. If your nails break easily, but you prefer their brighter sound, you can have them fortified at a nail salon. Some pickers use plastic or metal fingerpicks for their thumb and fingers to help create a bright sound. It's easiest to start with your bare fingers (or nails), but experiment with other methods to find the sound and feel that you prefer. All of the examples in the audio portion of this book were played with bare fingers and medium-length nails to provide a brighter attack.

 Tuning Notes

TRACK 1

4

SECTION I
GETTING STARTED

1 FINGERINGS AND STRING NUMBERS

Before we start, let's look at the standard labels for your fingers and your guitar's strings. Not only will this help you better understand this book, it also will help you understand most any other guitar book or video, since these conventions are used throughout the instructional-guitar community.

The Fretting Hand

Your *fretting hand* is the one that holds down the strings between frets on the neck of the guitar. Right-handed players use their *left hand* as the fretting hand. Here is a picture of the fretting hand holding down a chord:

In music notation, each of your fret-hand fingers is indicated by a number:

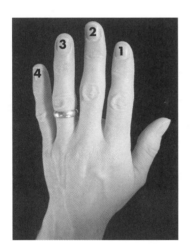

1 = index finger

2 = middle finger

3 = ring finger

4 = pinky finger

Here is how these fret-hand fingerings look in the context of a musical passage. Notice how the numbers are positioned near the notes in the music staff, not near the tablature notes below:

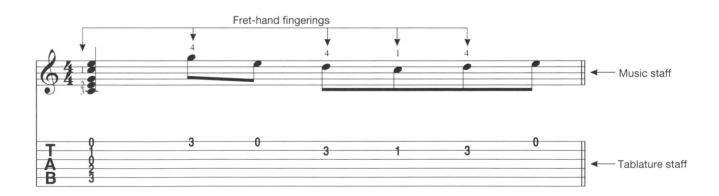

The Picking Hand

Your *picking hand* is the one you'll use to fingerpick the strings of your guitar. Right-handed players use their *right hand* to fingerpick the strings. Here is a picture of the picking hand resting on the guitar strings:

In music notation, each of your pick-hand fingers is indicated by a letter. At first glance, the following letters may seem like strange choices (we use "*p*" for "thumb" and "*a*" for "ring"?), but keep in mind that these letters are abbreviations for Spanish words, not English words:

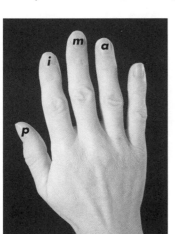

p = thumb ("pulgar")

i = index finger ("indice")

m = middle finger ("medio")

a = ring finger ("anular")

Here is how these pick-hand fingerings look in the context of a musical passage. Note how the fingerings are positioned between the music notation and tablature:

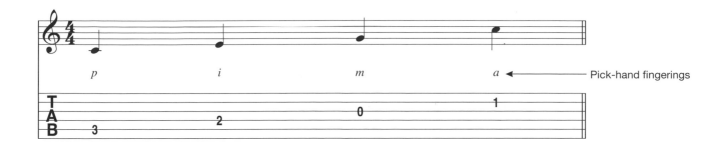

7

To help highlight and separate the thumb from the fingers, music notation often splits the parts, showing notes played by the thumb with stems pointing down and notes played with the fingers with stems pointing up:

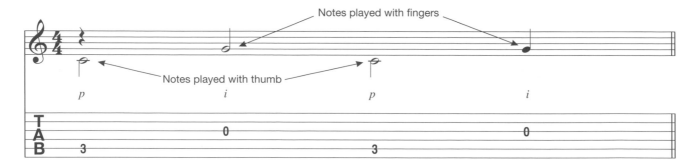

Guitar Strings

The six strings on your guitar are labeled from the highest string to the lowest string:

1 = high E string

2 = B string

3 = G string

4 = D string

5 = A string

6 = low E string

When you hold the guitar on your lap, notice that the highest-sounding string (the high E string) ends up closest to the ground, while the lowest-sounding string (the low E string) is the closest to the ceiling. This often confuses guitarists, since the highest string is "on the bottom" and the lowest string is "on the top," so it's important to keep this in mind when reading about string names/numbers.

SECTION II
ACCOMPANIMENT PATTERNS

2 FIRST PATTERN: THUMB-INDEX

Let's start by holding a G chord formation with our fretting hand. (If you haven't played a G chord before, see the shaded chord box below, which shows how to play a G chord.) Once your fingers are in place, place your picking-hand thumb on the sixth string (the lowest string). Then, slowly and steadily pluck that low string, which is the bass note of the G chord. Let's count along as we pluck that note. The example below has four beats in it, and we'll pluck the G note twice in each measure—every time we count the beats 1 and 3. When we're playing notes like this, that last for two beats, we're playing *half notes*.

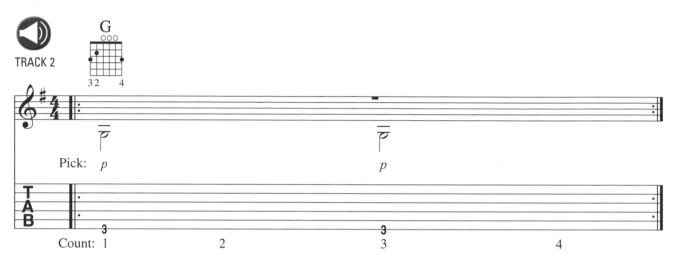

TRACK 2

Repeat this, slowly and steadily, until you feel comfortable playing it in time. If you have trouble feeling or counting the underlying beats, use a metronome, setting it to a slow tempo (about 60 bpm) and picking with your thumb on every other click. Then, gradually increase the speed of your metronome, making sure that you are playing the pattern cleanly before each speed increase, until you can play it at about 120 bpm.

The G Chord

Get your fretting hand in place for a G chord by placing your ring, middle, and pinky fingers on the sixth, fifth, and first strings, respectively. Both your ring and pinky fingers sit in the 3rd-fret space, while your middle finger sits in the 2nd-fret space. This is how a G chord looks:

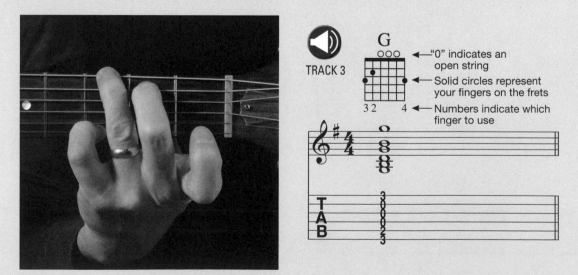

TRACK 3

← "0" indicates an open string

← Solid circles represent your fingers on the frets

← Numbers indicate which finger to use

Both the picture and the chord-grid graphic above represent the same thing, but notice how the chord-grid graphic is oriented in a different way. The picture shows what it looks like when you're standing in front of someone playing the G chord on the guitar. The strings in the picture are horizontal (parallel to the floor), while the chord grid shows how the chord shape looks on a vertically oriented guitar (imagine the guitar is in a stand, with its strings pointing up-and-down, perpendicular to the floor). To match up the picture and the graphic, you'll have to imagine one orientation or the other, rotating 90 degrees to match the two. This small discrepancy between the graphic and the picture often creates a lot of confusion, so, before moving on, take a close look at the two and make sure you can see how they both show the chord.

Once you have your fingers in place for the G chord, you're ready to test whether you have the strings fretted properly. Strum each string, one at a time, with your thumb or a finger, making sure that each note sounds clear. If you hear buzzing, adjust your fretting finger until the note sounds clear. To help eliminate buzzing, position your fretting fingers close to the frets that they are immediately behind.

Place your fingers directly behind each fret, as shown.

Do not place your fingers too far from the frets (as shown), as this can cause unwanted string buzz.

If you have small hands or have trouble fretting a G chord with the above fingering, here are two alternate fingerings you can try:

Now you're ready to add your index finger. Position your index finger just above the third string (you can even rest it right on the third string, if you like). Then, practice plucking the third string with your index finger a few times.

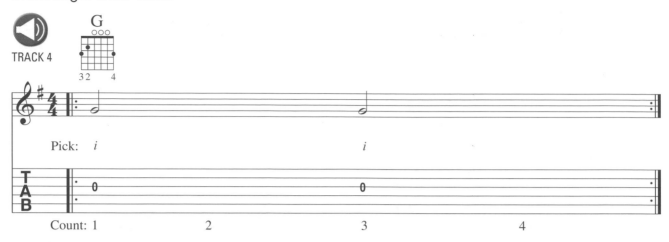

TRACK 4

Pick: *i*   *i*

Count: 1   2   3   4

TIP: Use Your Fingers as Reference Points on the Strings

If you have trouble plucking the correct string with your index finger, it might help to rest your middle and ring fingers on the second and first strings, respectively, to give your index finger a point of reference. Over time, you'll be able to lift those fingers off of the strings (your index finger will instinctively pluck the correct string without the aid of any extra points of reference).

Once you're comfortable with this motion, let's go back to our thumb pattern and alternate each thumb pick with an index-finger pluck. Count along: you'll pluck with your thumb every time you say "1" and "3"; you'll pluck with your index finger every time you say "2" and "4."

This next example contains a note with a solid notehead. This note is called a *quarter note* and gets one beat. The half notes (i.e., notes with empty noteheads) get two beats. (*For more information on how to read music notation, see the Appendix on page 51*).

TRACK 5

Pick: *p*   *i*   *p*   *i*

Count: 1   2   3   4

Try repeating this example for a while, like this:

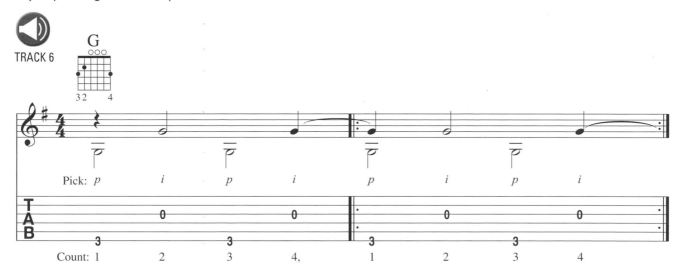

Again, if you have trouble, get out your metronome and practice the pattern at a slow speed, gradually increasing the tempo. You'll play a note with each click, alternating between your thumb and index finger: thumb, finger, thumb, finger, etc. Congratulations! You're already playing a fingerpicking pattern.

TIP: Why Am I Fretting Notes That I'm Not Playing?

At this point, you may notice that your fret hand is pushing down more notes than you're actually playing. Why do you need to hold down the fifth and first strings of the G chord when you're not playing them? The answer is that you *will* play more strings later on. Even though you're not playing those notes now, if you get your fret hand comfortable with holding down the whole chord, it will be much easier to pick more strings later. When you're comfortable holding down each chord, you won't have to think about your fretting hand; you'll only be thinking about which strings to pick.

You can use this exact same pattern for any six-string chord (a chord that uses all six strings on your guitar). Let's try it out on an E chord, for instance. (If you haven't played an E chord before, see the forthcoming chord box, which shows how to form an E chord):

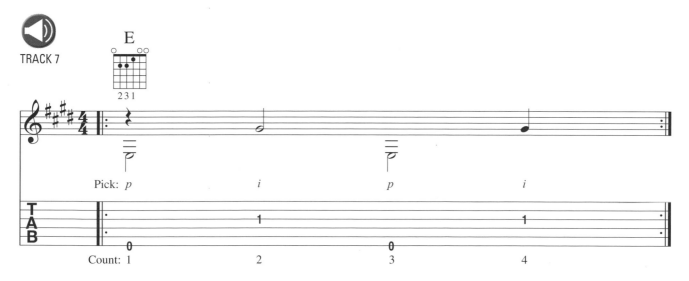

The E Chord

Get your fretting hand in place for an E chord by placing your middle, ring, and index fingers on the fifth, fourth, and third strings, respectively. Both your ring and middle fingers sit in the 2nd-fret space, while your index finger sits in the 1st-fret space. This is how an E chord looks:

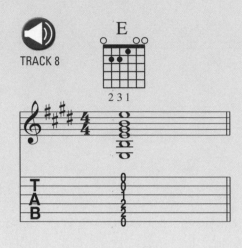

Just as you did with the G chord, test whether you have the strings fretted properly for the E chord by strumming each string, one at a time, with your thumb or a finger, making sure that each note sounds clear. If you hear buzzing, adjust your fretting finger until the note sounds clear.

Five-String Chords

Now that you have the first picking pattern down, it's easy to transfer it to other chords that use fewer strings. Let's try an A chord, which uses five strings. To pick the A chord, keep your index finger locked in place on the third string, but shift your thumb up to rest on the *fifth* string. Now pluck the same pattern—alternating between thumb and index-finger notes—but this time you'll be alternating between the fifth and third strings:

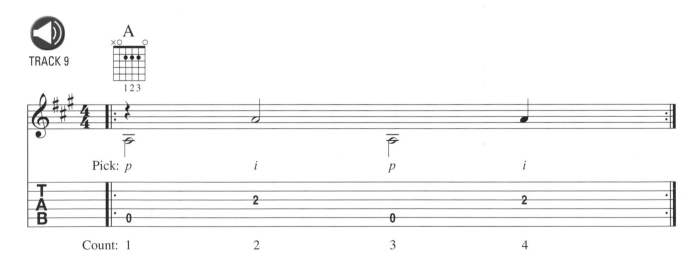

The A Chord

To play an A chord, you'll fret *all three* strings in the 2nd-fret space. Place your index, middle, and ring fingers on the fourth, third, and second strings, respectively (all behind the second fret). This is how an A chord looks:

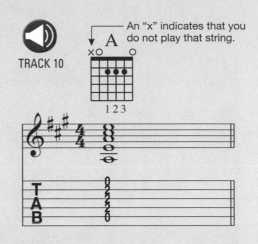

TRACK 10

An "x" indicates that you do not play that string.

Test whether you have the strings fretted properly for the A chord by strumming each string, one at a time, with your thumb or a finger, making sure that each note sounds clear. If you hear buzzing, adjust your fretting finger until the note sounds clear.

The previous fingering is just one way you can fret an A chord. Some players like to swap strings with their index and middle fingers (see picture on right), which can make changing between the A chord and some other chords a little easier. Try both ways, choosing the fingering you find most comfortable.

Once you have this pattern down, you can play any other five-string chord this way, too. Let's try a C chord now.

TRACK 11

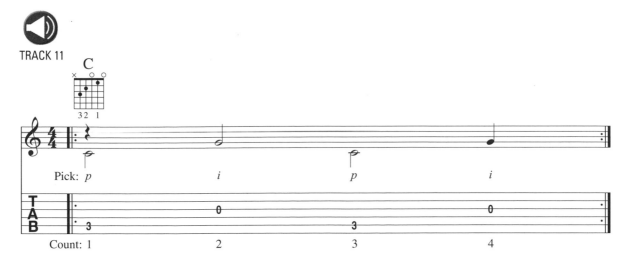

The C Chord

To play a C chord, place your ring, middle, and index fingers on the fifth, fourth, and second strings, respectively. For this chord, each finger will lay in a different fret space: your ring finger sits in the 3rd-fret space, your middle finger sits in the 2nd-fret space, and your index finger sits in the 1st-fret space. This is how a C chord looks:

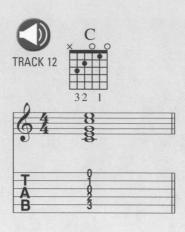

TRACK 12

Test whether you have the strings fretted properly for the C chord by strumming each string, one at a time, with your thumb or a finger, making sure that each note sounds clear. If you hear buzzing, adjust your fretting finger until the note sounds clear.

Changing Between Chords

Now that you can fingerpick a few different chords, the next step is to learn how to switch between chords. We'll try switching between E and A chords. Play one chord for two measures, then switch to the other chord, continuing to practice going back-and-forth until you can move between the chords and pick them fluidly. Remember that your index finger will pick the same string throughout, but you'll need to move your thumb from the sixth string (for the E chord) to the fifth string (for the A chord) and back again to the sixth string (as you move back to E).

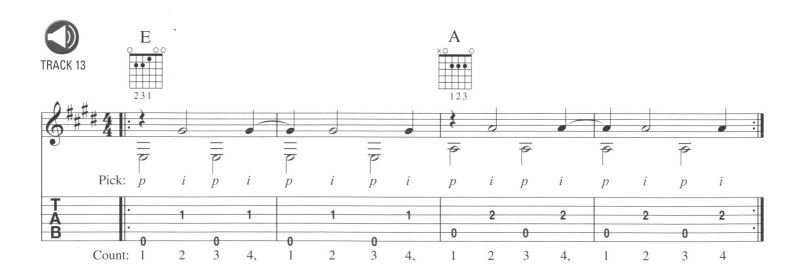

TIP: Changing Chords

Practice with a metronome and start as slowly as you need to so that you can switch chords and pluck the first note of the next chord without missing a beat. Don't worry if you need to slow things down to a crawl. It takes time to train your fingers to move from one chord to the next.

One trick to keep in mind is that for the first note in each chord (the first thumb pick), you're playing an open string. This means that you actually have a little extra time to get your fingers in place for the next chord, since that chord doesn't have to be completely fretted until you pluck the next note with your index finger.

Now let's try changing between the G and C chords. Just as you did when moving between the E and A chords, you'll have to shift your thumb from the sixth string (for the G chord) up to the fifth string (for the C chord).

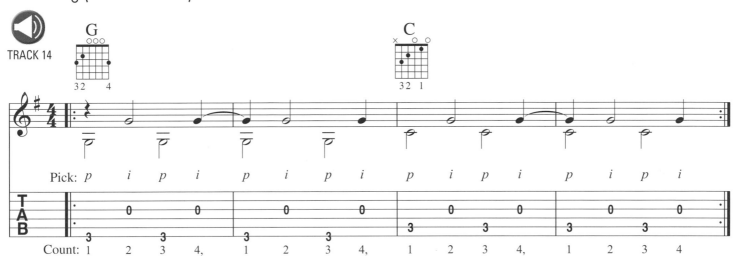

First Song: "Tom Dooley"

Now that we can fingerpick and change between chords, we have all the tools to play a song! Let's try the old folk tune "Tom Dooley." Here, we're just switching between A and E chords, like we did earlier in the chapter, except now we're starting with the A chord, instead of the E chord.

TIP: Singing and Playing Simultaneously

If you have trouble singing and playing "Tom Dooley," try separating the parts. First, practice the fingerpicked part until you can play it with chord changes, without thinking too much. Count along in your head and, if needed, tap your foot on each beat.

Then, learn the vocal part and sing it independently of the fingerpicked part. Make sure to mentally count along or tap your foot as you sing. You'll notice that many of the sung notes happen more quickly than the notes you're playing on the guitar. In fact, you'll often sing two notes for each beat or foot-tap. Listen to the accompanying recording to check your vocal rhythm (you also can learn the part by singing along, if you choose).

Once you have each part down individually, put them together, but make sure to play them at a much slower tempo than you were playing them individually. (And it's always good to practice with a metronome!) Once you can play them slowly, gradually increase your speed until you can sing and play the song at your desired tempo.

Four-String Chords

A good percentage of the chords that people play on the guitar have their bass note on either the sixth, fifth, or fourth string. So far, we've applied our picking pattern to chords that have bass notes on the sixth and fifth strings; therefore, once we know how to apply this pattern to chords that have their bass note on the fourth string, we'll be able to use the pattern with the vast majority of accompanimental chords.

You need to make just one small adjustement to play our pattern with a four-string chord: move your thumb up to the fourth string, leaving your index finger planted on the third string. Let's play a D chord using our pattern. Alternate between your thumb and index finger on the fourth and third strings, respectively:

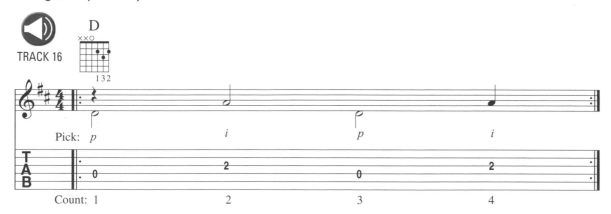

The D Chord

To play a D chord, place your index, ring, and middle fingers on the third, second, and first strings, respectively. For this chord, your index and middle fingers will occupy the 2nd-fret space, while your ring finger sits in the 3rd-fret space. This is how a D chord looks:

Test whether you have the strings fretted properly for the D chord by strumming each string, one at a time, with your thumb or a finger, making sure that each note sounds clear. If you hear buzzing, adjust your fretting finger until the note sounds clear.

Now that we can fingerpick a four-string chord, let's practice changing between all of our chord types. Let's start by moving between a six-string chord (G) and our four-string D chord. Your index finger will stay in the same place (on the third string), but pay attention to that thumb, which needs to move from the sixth string (for the G chord) all the way up to the fourth string (for the D chord), skipping the fifth string on its way.

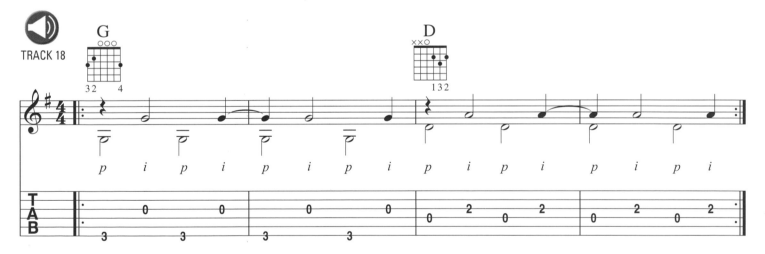

Next, let's try switching between three chords: G, C, and D. This will get us moving our thumb between all three bass-note strings: the sixth string (for the G chord), the fifth string (for the C chord), and the fourth string (for the D chord). Take your time on the following example, since this is the first time you'll be switching chords every measure (twice as fast as we've previously been changing chords). Remember to work with your metronome if you have problems, starting at a slow enough tempo to make the chord changes cleanly in time, then gradually increase the speed by a few metronome clicks each time until you can play the example at the medium pace at which it's played on the accompanying track.

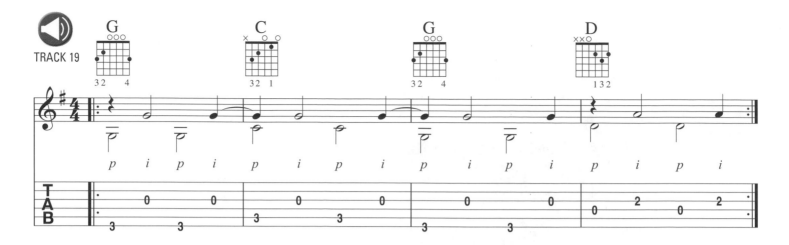

"Summer Days"

You already have all the tools to play many songs! You may have even heard some that use picking patterns similar to what we've already learned. One great example is the White Stripes' "We're Going to Be Friends," which uses a similar picking pattern and mostly G, C, and D chords throughout. The following tune, "Summer Days," uses picking patterns and phrases reminiscent of this White Stripes hit. The chords change slowly throughout the first eight measure of the tune, but things speed up in measures 9–11, where you move up to a D chord, then move to C for just one measure before going back to G. If you have trouble with these quick chord changes, remember to slow things down and play with a metronome. Isolate just these few measures, repeating them until you're comfortable moving from D to C to G.

Words and Music by
Andrew DuBrock

3 MIDDLE-FINGER PATTERNS

Now that we're comfortable picking with our thumb and index finger, let's gradually work in the middle finger. Adding this finger into our patterns will enable us to play one more string of each chord—your index finger plucks notes on the third string, while your middle finger plucks notes on the second string.

Let's start with our familiar G chord. Fret the G chord with your fretting hand, and position your pick-hand thumb and fingers so that your thumb, index, middle, and ring fingers rest on the sixth, third, second, and first strings, respectively. Before we pick a pattern, let's try the middle finger on its own a few times, just as we did with the index finger in the previous chapter:

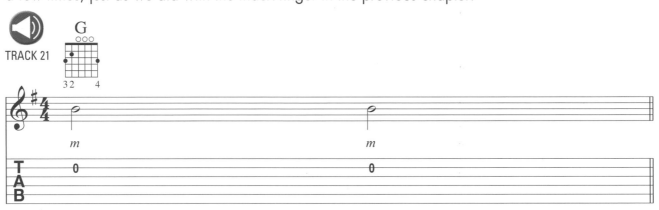

Now we'll alternate between our thumb and middle fingers, playing beats 1 and 3 with our thumb and alternating on beats 2 and 4 with our middle finger.

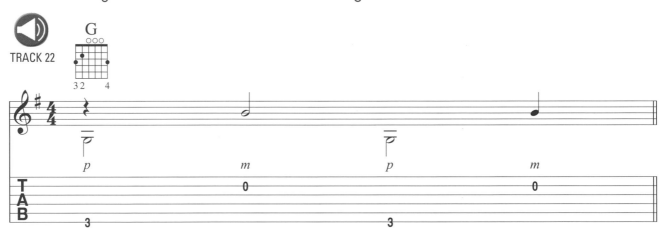

Let's try our pattern on another six-string chord. This time, let's try E minor. (If you haven't played an Em chord before, see the forthcoming chord box, which illustrates how to fret this chord.)

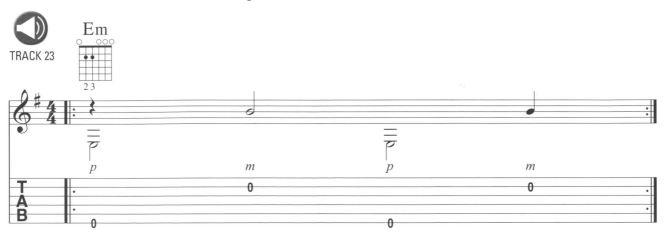

The Em Chord

To play an Em chord, place your middle and ring fingers in the 2nd-fret space of the fifth and fourth strings, respectively. This is how the Em chord looks:

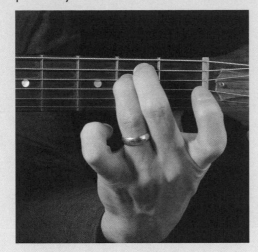

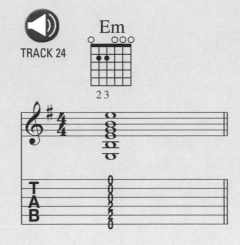

TRACK 24

Five- and Four-String Chords with the Thumb–Middle Pattern

Now let's practice our pattern on a few five- and four-string chords. For our five-string chord, let's play Am (see chord box below, if you haven't played this chord before). To pick any five-string chord like this, keep your middle finger on the second string, shifting your thumb up to the fifth string for the bass note of the chord.

TRACK 25

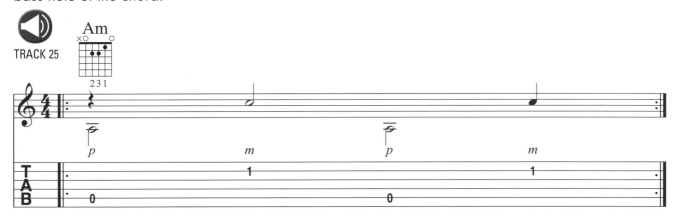

The Am Chord

To play an Am chord, place your middle and ring fingers in the 2nd-fret space of the fourth and third strings, respectively, and place your index finger in the 1st-fret space of the second string. This is how the Am chord looks:

TRACK 26

Transferring this pattern to a four-string chord is easy, too. Just like we did with the thumb-index pattern, all you need to do is move your thumb up to the fourth string, while your middle finger stays on the second string. We'll try a four-string thumb-middle picking pattern with a D minor chord:

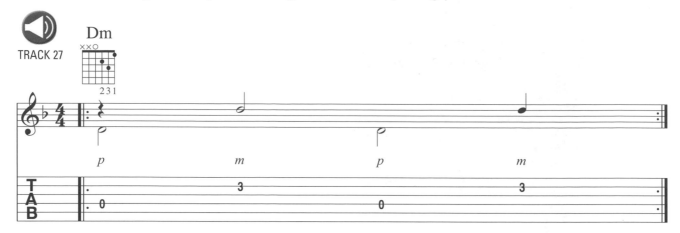

The Dm Chord

To play a Dm chord, place your middle finger in the 2nd-fret space of the third string, your ring finger in the 3rd-fret space of the second string, and your index finger in the 1st-fret space of the first string. This is how a Dm chord looks:

Let's try one more four-string chord: the F chord.

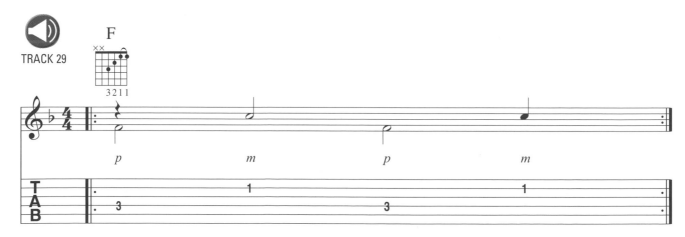

The F Chord

To play an F chord, place your ring finger in the 3rd-fret space of the fourth string and your middle finger in the 2nd-fret space of the third string. Then barre your index finger across the top two strings, at the 1st fret ("barre" means to flatten your finger across more than one string so that you fret multiple strings with one finger). This is how an F chord looks:

This is one of the most difficult chords that we've played, since you have to fret every note of the chord and barre across the top two strings with your index finger. Because of this, don't worry if you need extra time to get this chord under your fingers. Make sure to strum the chord slowly to help detect any buzzing. If you hear some, readjust your fingers so that the strings ring clearly.

TIP: It's Not Always About How Hard You Press, but Rather *Where* You Press

If you're having trouble with the F chord, take a break and relax before you start pressing the strings down so hard that your fingers cramp! It's natural to think that you have to press down the strings harder if a chord buzzes, but, in many cases, it's more about where you're applying the pressure, than how hard you're pressing (and pressing too hard can lead to problems like carpal tunnel or tendonitis, so be careful!). Here are a few things you might try to help make any chord sound clearer:

Place your finger close to the fret. As we discussed earlier in this book, it's easier to hold strings down when your fingers are closer to the frets. If you're looking at the fret space, your finger should be closer to the fret that's near the soundhole of the guitar, not the fret that's closer to the tuning pegs of the guitar.

Experiment with finger placement. When fretting more than one string on the same fret (with different fingers; for example, an A chord), it's impossible to get all fingers up against the fret. But you can still experiment with your finger placement on chords like this to make sure you have your fingers in the most efficient places.

Only apply pressure where it's needed. For barre chords in which one finger frets more than one string, remember that your finger needs to hold down only the strings that other fingers aren't fretting. On the F chord, people often lay their fingers across more than just the first two strings, but those are the only two strings to which you need to apply enough pressure for the strings to sound.

Now you're ready to apply this picking pattern to complete chord progressions and songs. To get you started, let's try this eight-measure chord progression, which sounds like it could be the foundation of a folk- or classic-rock song:

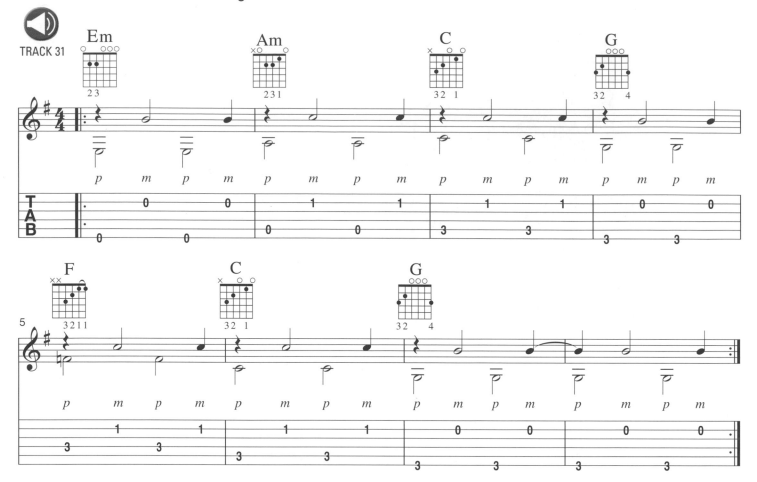

Mixing Middle- and Index-Finger Patterns

When playing the thumb-index pattern, you may notice that it occasionally can sound a little thin on some chords. The thumb-index pattern utilizes only two notes of any chord, so one way that you can thicken the sound of your chords is by adding more strings into your fingerpicking patterns. We can do this now by mixing thumb-middle and thumb-index patterns. This will help thicken the sound because, by adding one more string, we're also adding another chord tone.

Let's try this out with a G chord. First, play a thumb-middle pattern on beats 1 and 2, then move to a thumb-index pattern on beats 3 and 4. Your thumb plays the same notes it always has—on beats 1 and 3—but your middle and index fingers alternate between the other two beats, with your middle finger plucking on beat 2 and your index finger plucking on beat 4.

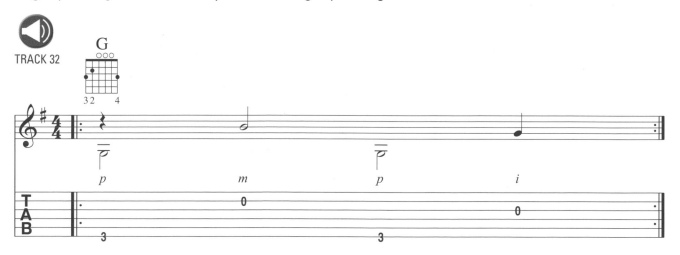

Once you're comfortable with this pattern on a G chord, try it out on an A minor chord. For your picking hand, the only change from the G chord will be moving your thumb up to the fifth string.

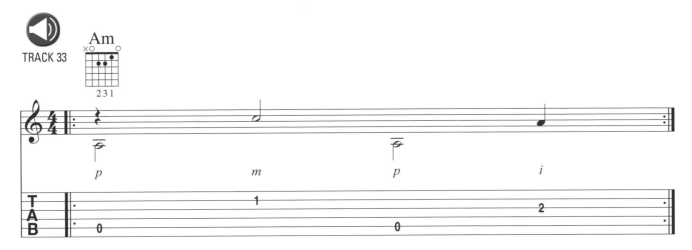

Now that we've tried our "mixed" pattern on six- and five-string chords, let's take it for a spin on a four-string chord—D minor. All you need to do (aside from fretting the Dm chord) is shift your thumb up to the fourth string—your index and middle fingers stay parked on the third and second strings, respectively:

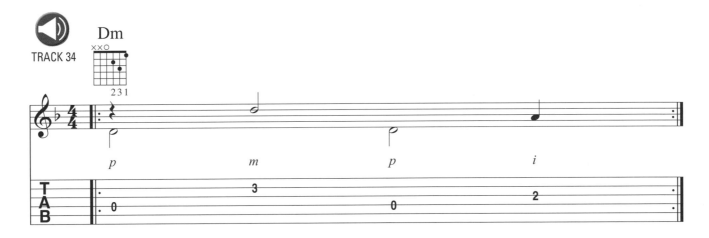

Let's finish this chapter by playing the song "Summer Days" with our new pattern that alternates between thumb-middle and thumb-index picking patterns. As you can see, this pattern fills out the chord a little more throughout the song, and it sounds a lot more like the accompaniment that Jack White uses in the White Stripes' "We're Going to Be Friends."

SUMMER DAYS

Words and Music by
Andrew DuBrock

4 ADDING THE RING FINGER

At this point, you're comfortable using your thumb, index, and middle fingers in fingerpicking patterns. That's quite an accomplishment! Some fingerpickers (even some famous ones) spend their whole careers picking patterns with just two fingers—their thumb and index finger. But the more fingers you can use to pick patterns, the more varied your patterns can be. Thus, we can expand our options even more by training our ring finger to pick patterns, as well.

Let's start again with our old, familiar G chord. Get your fret-hand fingers in place and rest your picking hand on the strings, with your thumb, index, middle, and ring fingers on the sixth, third, second, and first strings, respectively. To get comfortable using your ring finger, practice plucking the first string with it.

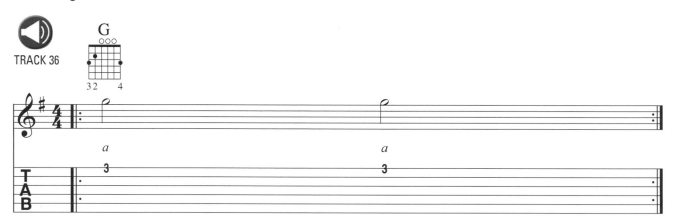

Next, we'll alternate between the thumb (on the sixth string) and the ring finger (on the first string), like this:

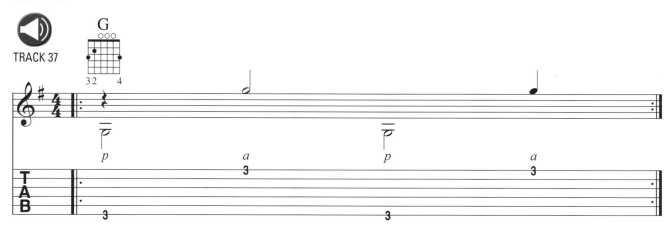

Let's try this pattern on another six-string chord, E7.

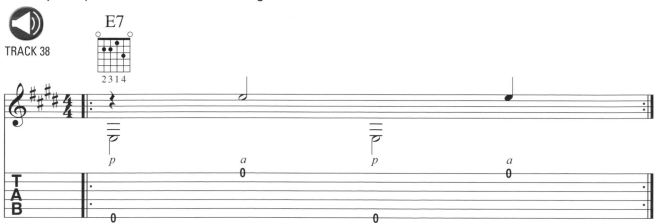

The E7 Chord

To play an E7 chord, start by playing an E chord, with your middle and ring fingers in the 2nd-fret space of the fifth and fourth strings, respectively, and your index finger in the 1st-fret space of the third string. Then add your pinky to the 3rd-fret space of the second string. Here is how an E7 chord looks:

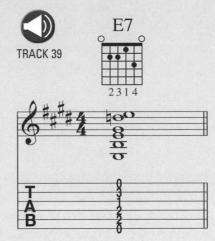

Many different versions of every chord exist. For instance, there's another very common (and easier) way to play the E7 chord in this position. Simply start with a standard E chord and remove your ring finger from the 2nd fret of the fourth string. This version of the E7 chord looks like this:

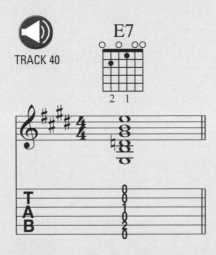

While this version is easier to play, we're going to use the first version for now because it works better with the fingerpicking patterns that we're learning. (If you want to know why the second version doesn't work as well, see the forthcoming TIP box: Why Does This E7 Chord Sound the Same as a Regular E Chord When I Use the Thumb-Ring Pattern?)

TIP: Why Does This E7 Chord Sound the Same as a Regular E Chord When I Use the Thumb-Ring Pattern?

You may have noticed that when you're fingerpicking the E7 chord, it sounds exactly the same as an E chord. Let's compare the two, to see what I mean. In the next example, pick an E chord for two measures, then add your pinky to play the E7 chord for two measures.

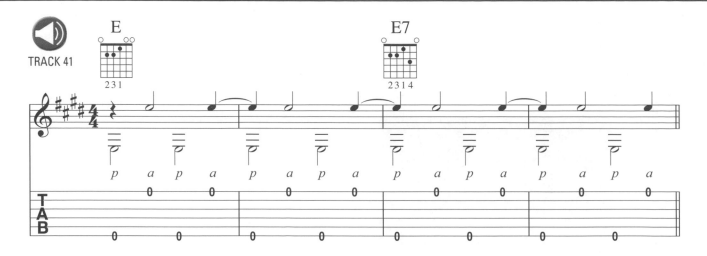

Notice how the only note that changed between these two chords is on the second string, and you're not even picking that string! So, then, why are we even learning the picking pattern with this E7 chord? Simple—because your fingers need to get comfortable with fretting the chord while picking, and right now you're learning to fingerpick with the thumb-ring pattern (and, in the process, learning this new E7 shape, too). Check out what happens when you play these chords with a thumb-middle picking pattern, instead:

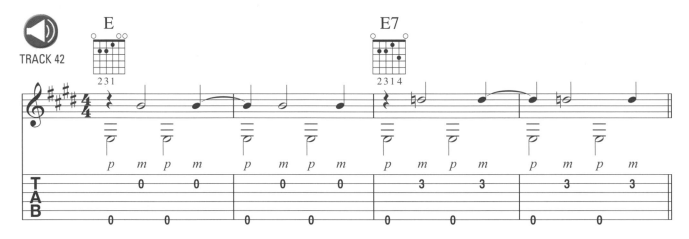

Now you can hear the difference between these two chords! Later on, we'll start using even more patterns with this chord, but for now, we need to make sure we can fret the chord shape while playing the thumb-ring picking pattern.

Another question you may have is: Why don't we use the second, easier version of the E7 chord shape, as shown in the E7 chord sidebar? To show you why, let's compare this E7 shape to a standard E chord, using all three of our finger combinations: thumb-index, thumb-middle, and thumb-ring.

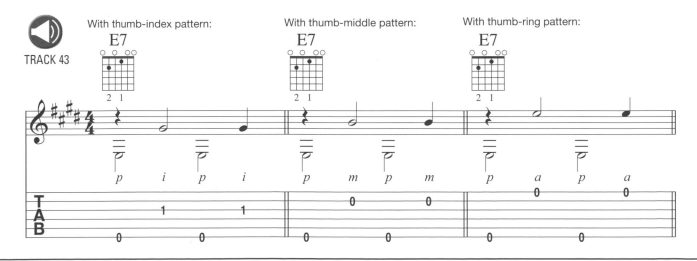

Did you notice that both of these chords, E and E7, sound exactly the same for each of our fingerpicking patterns? That's because the note that gives this chord its name (the "7th" in the E7 chord) is on the fourth string, and our picking patterns don't use that string when playing a six-string chord shape. This is why we'll use the other E7 shape for now. Later on, in the "Alternate-Bass Fingerpicking" section, we'll learn a pattern that works with this easier version of the E7 chord, and as your playing develops, you'll learn plenty of fingerpicking patterns that work with this chord shape.

Five- and Four-String Chords with the Thumb-Ring Pattern

Now let's get comfortable playing our thumb-ring pattern with some five- and four-string chords. Let's utilize two five-string chords—A7 and B7. For these chords, all we need to do is move the thumb on our picking hand up to the fifth string, leaving our ring finger on the first string (similar to what we did for the thumb-index and thumb-middle patterns):

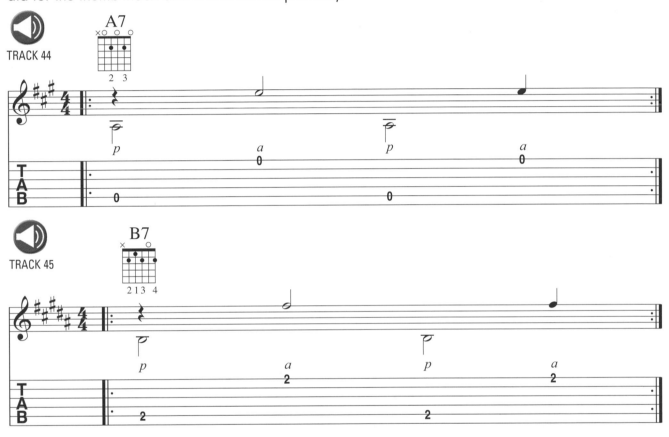

TRACK 44

TRACK 45

The A7 Chord

To play an A7 chord, place your middle and ring fingers in the 2nd-fret space of the fourth and second strings, respectively. This is how the A7 chord looks:

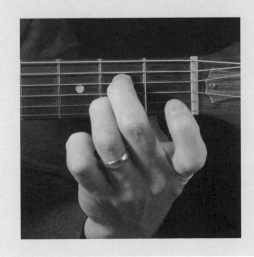

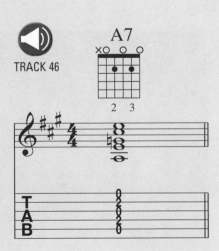

TRACK 46

A7

The B7 Chord

To play a B7 chord, place your middle, ring, and pinky fingers in the 2nd-fret space of the fifth, third, and first strings, respectively; then place your index finger in the 1st-fret space of the fourth string. This is how the B7 chord looks:

TRACK 47

This four-fingered chord is quite hard to grab, so make sure each string sounds properly, adjusting any fingers, if necessary.

For four-string chords, simply move the thumb on your picking hand up to the fourth string, leaving your ring finger on the first string. Let's try a D7 chord:

TRACK 48

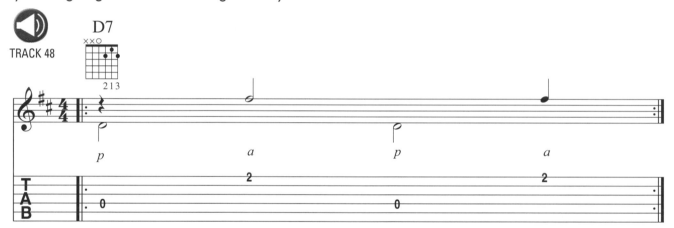

The D7 Chord

To play a D7 chord, place your middle and ring fingers in the 2nd-fret space of the third and first strings, respectively; then place your index finger in the 1st-fret space of the second string. This is how the D7 chord looks:

TRACK 49

Playing the Blues

One great way to practice seventh chords is by playing blues songs, because blues songs often use a lot of seventh chords. We'll play the traditional blues song "Alberta," using E7, A7, and B7 chords. To make things more interesting, let's mix our patterns. In the previous chapter, we alternated the thumb-middle picking pattern with the thumb-index pattern, so let's do the same thing with our new thumb-ring pattern. We'll alternate the thumb-ring pattern with the thumb-index pattern here, getting comfortable with it by practicing this alternating pattern over the E7, A7, and B7 chords:

Now let's work these patterns into our song. "Alberta" uses the most common blues progression—the 12-bar blues. The basic structure of this progression starts with E7 for four measures, then moves to A7 for two measures before returning to E7 for two more measures. The structure then finishes by moving to B7 for two measures and concluding with two measures of E7.

ALBERTA

Traditional
Arranged by Andrew DuBrock

SECTION III

MOVING ON

5 PUTTING IT ALL TOGETHER: MIXING FINGER COMBINATIONS

You now possess all the necessary tools to create a multitude of fingerpicking patterns. All you need to do is take your thumb-index, thumb-middle, and thumb-ring patterns and mix them up and blend them together into a pattern you like for any given song or chord progression. In this chapter, we'll practice mixing these patterns in different ways while also looking at a few concepts that should help you decide which pattern to use in any situation.

Choose Picking Patterns That Highlight the Chords You're Using

When we played "Alberta" in the last chapter, our picking pattern sounded pretty good, but can we make it even better? Let's look at the pattern once more and see how it relates to each chord. All of our chords are seventh chords, and those "7ths" are what give the chords their flavors. That colorful note falls on the third string for both the A7 and B7 chords, but it falls on the *second* string for the E7 chord. Here's the picking pattern that we used over all three chords:

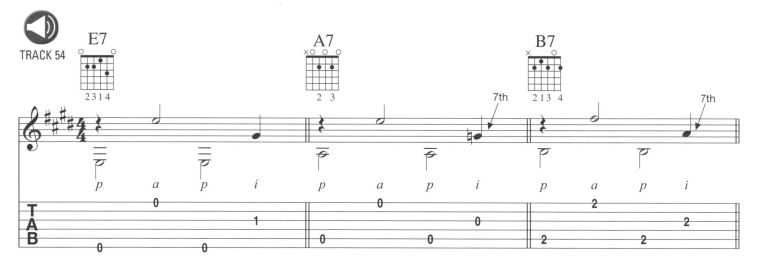

Notice how we play that colorful note, the 7th, for the A7 and B7 chords when we pluck the third string, but we never play the second string for the E7 chord, where the 7th is located. So, if we want to include this note in all of our chords, let's try alternating between thumb-middle and thumb-index combinations. Here's how this works for each chord:

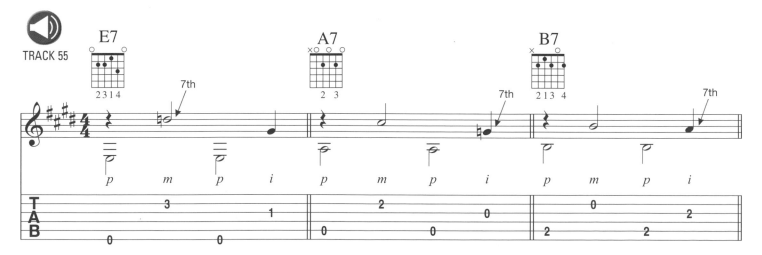

This pattern sounds great for all chords, so let's try it with "Alberta":

ALBERTA

TRACK 56

Traditional
Arranged by Andrew DuBrock

Oh, Al - ber - ta,___ where'd you stay last night? Oh, Al -

ber - ta,___ where'd you stay last night? Came home this

morn - ing,___ sun was shin - ing bright.

TIP: Use Picking Patterns That Highlight Colorful Notes in a Chord

When coming up with a pattern for our E7, A7, and B7 chords, we looked at what strings the colorful "7th" note appeared on for each chord. But you don't have to know any theory to know what sounds good. When you're working with a song or chord progression of your own, try picking different string combinations and listen carefully. Your ear will know which one sounds best—and sometimes there will be more than one string combination that sounds great. Trust your ear and pick the patterns that sound best to you.

You can also swap the "building blocks" of your fingerpicking pattern. For instance, instead of using the thumb-middle, thumb-index pattern (with the middle-finger pattern coming first), try a thumb-index, thumb-middle pattern, like this:

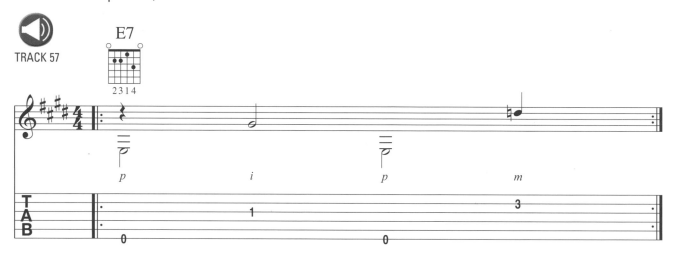

Mix All the Fingers into Larger Picking Patterns

So far, we've mixed two picking patterns together—whether it's the thumb-index and thumb-middle, the thumb-index and thumb-ring, or any combination thereof. But you can craft larger picking patterns and phrases, too. There's really no limit to how you can put these patterns together. For instance, we can play a measure of thumb-index, thumb-middle, and follow that up with a measure of thumb-index, thumb-ring, like this:

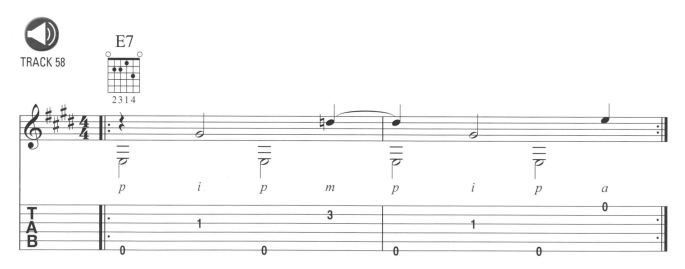

Practice that example until you're comfortable with it, then try using it in a full song (you can even try it with "Alberta").

Another variation that you can try is a measure of thumb-ring, thumb-middle, followed by a measure of thumb-ring, thumb-index. As you can see, there are plenty of ways to mix these patterns together:

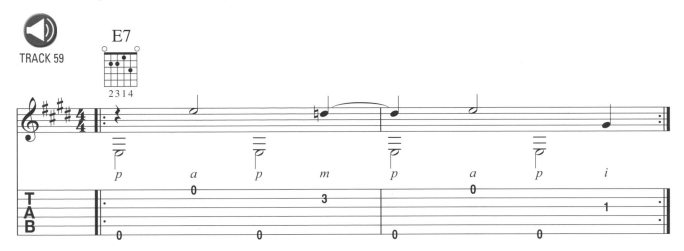

Another way to mix up your pattern is to play a measure of thumb-index, thumb-middle, followed by a measure of thumb-ring, thumb-middle. This creates a free-flowing pattern because we're moving from our index to our middle to our ring fingers, then doubling back through the middle finger and repeating the whole process. To fully understand this concept, try repeating this pattern a few times:

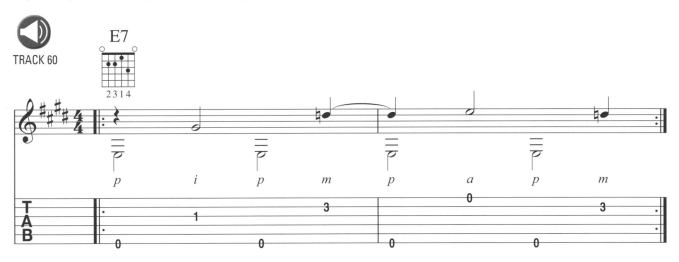

TIP: Create Your Own Patterns!

Now you're ready to come up with your own picking patterns. Use the tools we've learned so far to craft patterns that you like for your own songs and chord progressions.

Let's finish this chapter by playing through "Alberta" with the free-flowing pattern that we just learned.

ALBERTA

TRACK 61

Traditional
Arranged by Andrew DuBrock

6 THE NEXT STEP: ALTERNATE-BASS FINGERPICKING

You already possess the tools to play many fingerpicking patterns, and you're only two small steps away from being able to play arguably the most popular fingerpicking pattern of all time—alternate-bass fingerpicking (sometimes called "Travis picking").

Let's start with a measure of thumb-middle, thumb-index and work up to our new pattern. We'll use an E7 chord, but notice that this is the easier-to-fret version of the E7 chord—not the one we've been using (if you need to review this version of the chord, turn back to Chapter 4).

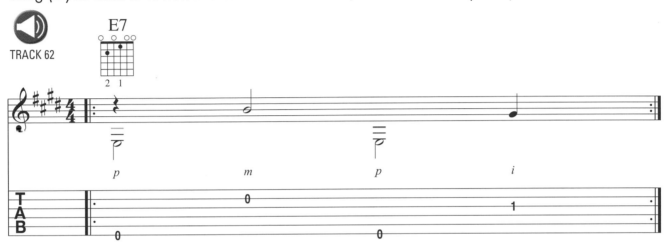

Now let's play exactly the same pattern, but this time move your pick-hand thumb up to grab the open fourth string on beat 3. If you have trouble with this, imagine that you're simply shifting to a four-string chord (for example, a D chord) in the middle of the measure. But, while the thumb of your picking hand moves up to the fourth string, your other hand still frets the same E7 chord.

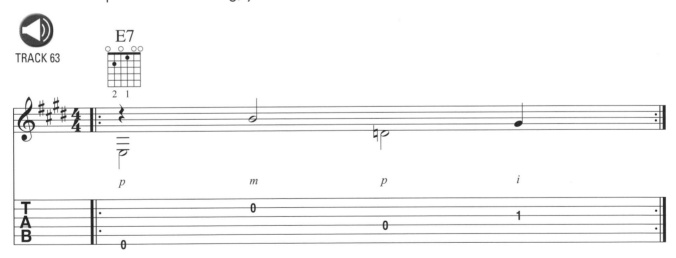

Repeat this pattern, practicing it until your thumb feels comfortable jumping back-and-forth between the sixth and fourth strings. This jump between bass notes ("alternate" bass notes) is what gives "alternate-bass fingerpicking" its name. We're also playing the note that gives that E7 chord its unique sound—the 7th, which appears on the open fourth string. We're now playing the easier version of the E7 chord because we still get the chord's unique character when playing this new fingerpicking pattern.

At this point, you're playing alternate-bass fingerpicking, but most people play the pattern twice as fast as the speed at which we've been playing it (actually, the speed is dictated by the musical context, but it always *looks* twice as fast, and it will be twice as fast in the following example). To do this, simply double the pattern, playing a bass note on *every* beat (instead of every two beats). Consequently, all of the notes played by your fingers will fall *between* the beats. You count this by adding an "&" in between each beat ("1 &, 2 &, 3 &, 4 &").

TIP: Eighth Notes

So far, we've only played *quarter notes*. If you divide a quarter note into two equal parts, you get two *eighth notes*. So, now we're playing every eighth-note subdivision in each measure, with the eighth notes between each beat getting the "&" count.

That's it! You're now playing a complete alternate-bass fingerpicking pattern. Now all we have to do is apply that to whatever chord we want to play. For any six-string chord, we can use the pattern that we just played with our E7 chord. Let's try the pattern with a G chord. Make sure to count along, if you need to.

TIP: Use Your Metronome

If you're having trouble getting the feel of this alternate-bass fingerpicking, remember to use your metronome. To make it easier, start by setting your metronome to play on every eighth-note subdivision—meaning it will click eight times in each measure. Then practice playing one note per click; with the metronome set this way, every thumb and finger note will play on a click. Once you're comfortable with this, slow your metronome down a bit and play only thumb-picked notes when it clicks; in this case, each of the notes you pluck with your fingers will fall *between* consecutive clicks.

Alternate Between the Fifth and Fourth Strings for Five-String Chords

For six-string chords, we used our thumb to alternate between the sixth and fourth strings—jumping the fifth string each time. But our pattern for five-string chords has the thumb moving between adjacent strings; here, the thumb alternates between the fifth and fourth strings. Let's try this with an A7 chord:

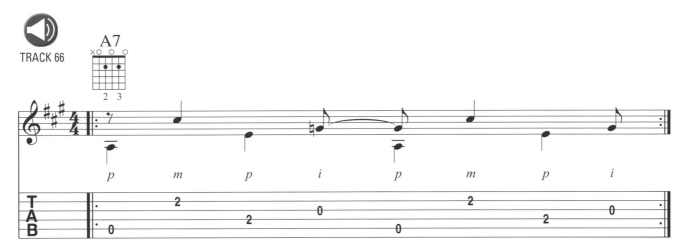

Any five-string chord should work with this pattern. Let's try B7:

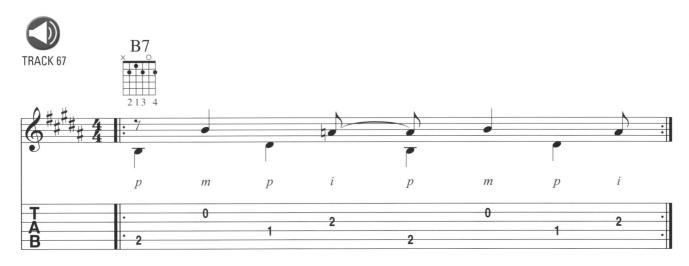

Now that you have the alternate-bass fingerpicking pattern down for five- and six-string chords, let's see how "Alberta" sounds with our new pattern. Remember to play the easier E7 chord, and notice how picking twice as fast really fills out the accompaniment pattern.

ALBERTA

Traditional
Arranged by Andrew DuBrock

Oh, Al - ber - ta,_____ where'd you stay last

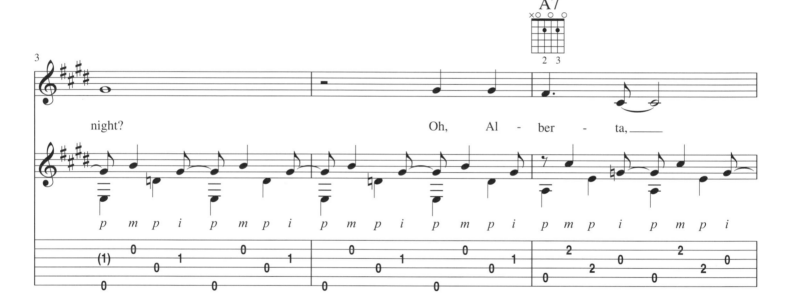

night? Oh, Al - ber - ta,_____

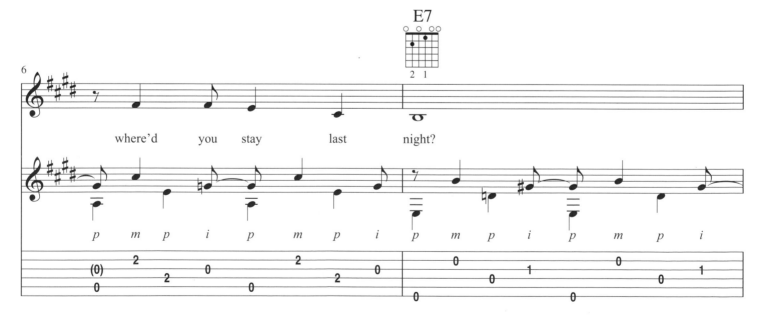

where'd you stay last night?

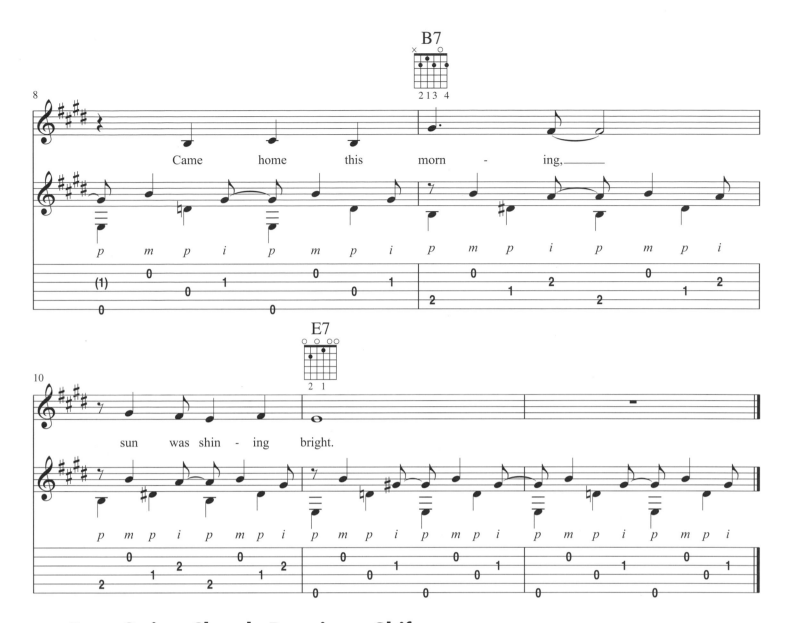

Four-String Chords Require a Shift

When we play four-string chords with alternate-bass fingerpicking, we get one more wrinkle. Here, we'll alternate our thumb between the fourth and third strings. It sounds fine at first, but remember that we've parked our index fingers on the third string throughout the entire course of this book! So, where does that finger go? It moves up one string (to the second string), and your middle finger moves up a string, too (to the first string). Consequently, your ring finger gets bumped off of the strings, but we won't need it for picking these four-string chords with the current pattern, however.

If this explanation sounds a little confusing, just imagine that you're picking the five-string A7 chord, but shifting *all* of your fingers up one string—including your thumb. This pattern should work with any four-string chord on the top four strings. Here's how it looks with a Dm chord:

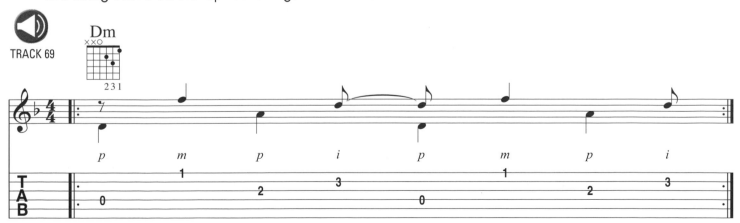

Adapt Patterns, When Necessary

For our final exploration, always remember that music is not written in stone—you can manipulate these patterns yourself. Don't be afraid to change things if it works better within the context of a song. For instance, let's try playing the traditional tune "Shady Grove," which shifts between Dm and C chords.

We've already played our pattern using a Dm chord, so let's try out a C chord with our alternate-bass fingerpicking pattern. This is a five-string chord, so we'll use the pattern that we learned earlier in this chapter:

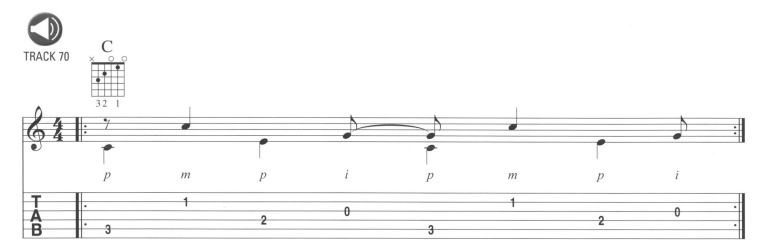

This pattern sounds fine on a C chord, and it works great for many songs, but notice what happens when we start changing between Dm and C chords:

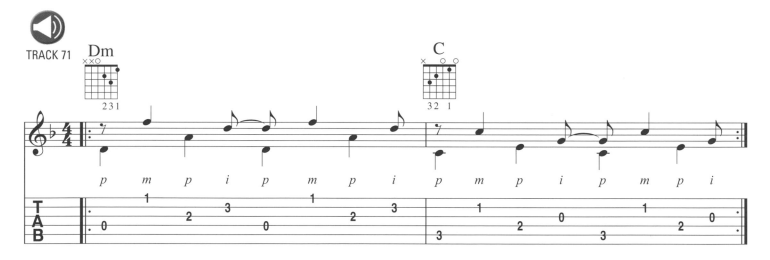

What happened? While shifting from the Dm chord to the C chord, all of your fingers (including your thumb) have to move down one string, and then you have to shift them all back up again to play the Dm when the phrase repeats! If you found this a bit tricky, you're not the only one. And, while it may work okay, it *sounds* a little jumpy, too.

One way to smooth out this pattern a bit is to keep your fingers on the top four strings for the C chord. That way, we'll still be playing notes on the first string when we're picking our C chord. But we still want to play that low bass note for the C chord, which is down on the fifth string. Therefore, our compromise will be to play notes on the first two strings with our fingers (middle and index), but to alternate between the *fifth* and *third* strings with our thumb (instead of the fifth and fourth strings).

48

Here's how that pattern sounds:

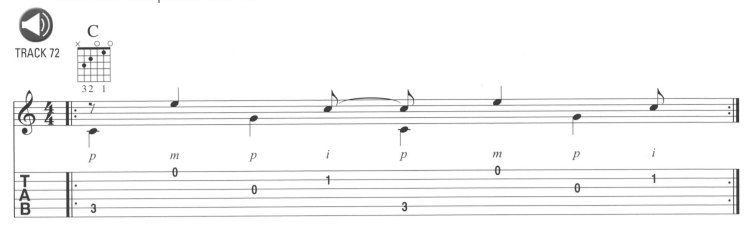

This already may feel comfortable to you because it's actually the same pattern that we played for six-string chords—we just moved the whole thing up one string (your thumb alternates between the fifth and third strings, instead of the sixth and fourth strings).

Now when we change between our Dm and C chords, notice how much smoother it sounds:

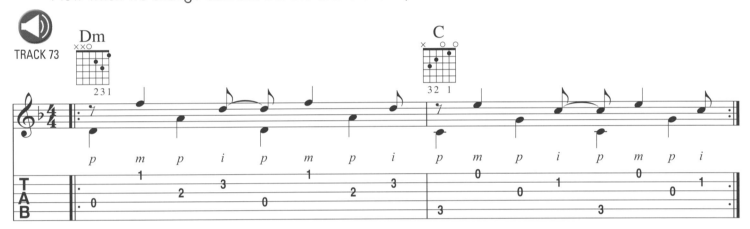

Now we're ready for our final song: "Shady Grove." The trickiest part of this song involves the quick chord changes in the final two measures. Here, we play each chord for only *half* a measure. Make sure to slow this section down, if you need to, and remember to use that metronome!

SHADY GROVE

Traditional
Arranged by Andrew DuBrock

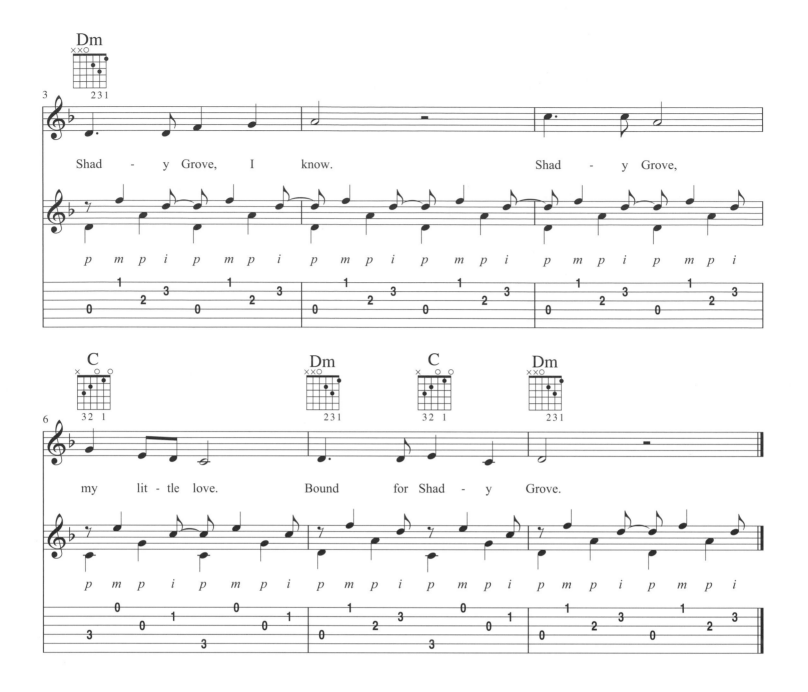

Congratulations!

You can now fingerpick one of the most popular patterns ever played on guitar. If you want to continue studying alternate-bass fingerpicking, you're ready for the next step. *Travis Picking*, by Andrew DuBrock (published by Hal Leonard), can teach you how to expand this pattern into accompanimental patterns like Paul Simon used in some of his most famous tunes. You'll also learn how to use these patterns to pick solo tunes like your acoustic blues heroes, and more advanced patterns like those played by Nashville greats Merle Travis and Chet Atkins.

If you'd like to broaden your studies to include not only fingerpicking, but also strummed rhythm and lead guitar, *Total Acoustic Guitar*, by Andrew DuBrock (published by Hal Leonard), is a great place to start. For more information on either of these books, please visit *andrewdubrock.com*.

APPENDIX

The following information provides a brief overview of some basic music theory concepts. To learn more on this topic, check out *Music Theory, A Practical Guide for All Musicians* (Hal Leonard).

READING MUSIC

In music notation, horizontal lines and the spaces in between them are used to represent notes. Each grouping consists of five horizontal lines, which is called the *staff*. The notes on each staff are determined by a symbol at the beginning of the staff, called the *clef*. While there are many clefs, by far the most common one is the *treble clef*. This is the one used for guitar music.

As shown below, the lines on this staff represent the following notes, in ascending order: E, G, B, D, and F. You can use an acronym to help you remember these notes (e.g., "Every Good Boy Deserves Fudge"). The notes in the spaces between each line are, in ascending order: F, A, C, and E ("FACE"). Notes may be placed above or below the staff, too. To add notes outside of the staff, we use short horizontal lines called *ledger lines*. Here are the notes on the staff:

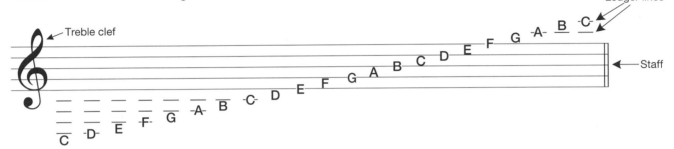

Music notation uses solid and hollow circles (technically, ovals) and lines to represent notes and their respective lengths. A hollow circle with no lines attached is a whole note, which gets four beats. In 4/4 time, the most common *time signature* (see the forthcoming section on Time Signatures for more information), a whole note fills an entire measure:

A hollow circle with a *stem* attached (a vertical line) is a *half note*, which gets two beats. Two half notes fit in each measure in 4/4 time:

A solid circle with a stem attached is a *quarter note*, which gets one beat. It takes four quarter notes to fill one measure in 4/4 time:

A solid circle that has a stem with a *flag* is an eighth note. On a single eighth note, a flag is a curvy line (shown below). When more than one eighth note is grouped together, their flags are often joined by *beams*. A single measure can contain as many as eight eighth notes in 4/4 time:

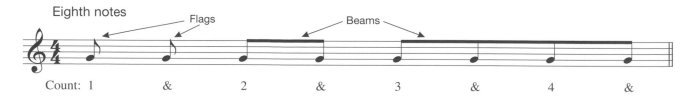

A solid circle that has a stem with a *double flag* is a sixteenth note. A single measure can contain as many as sixteen sixteenth notes in 4/4 time:

TIME SIGNATURES

Appearing at the beginning of a piece, the *time signature* indicates the meter for the song. Time signatures consist of two numbers stacked on top of each other. The top number tells you how many beats are in each measure, and the bottom number tells you what the note value is for each beat. To get the correct beat value for the bottom number, you have to pretend it's the bottom number of a fraction in which the number "1" is on top. For instance, the following time signature—4/4— indicates four beats per measure, with a quarter note (1/4) receiving one beat.

"Four-four" time is the most common time signature, and you'll often see a "C" in place of the "4/4" marking ("C" stands for "common time"):

Waltzes, as well as many other three-beat songs, use a 3/4 time signature, which has three quarter-note beats per measure:

In 6/8 time, each measure contains six beats, with each *eighth note* receiving one beat:

In 6/8 time, however, the beats are often grouped into two sets of three notes. In this case, although there *are* six beats per measure, the beats are often counted *one*-and-ah, *two*-and-ah, instead of *one*-two-three, *four*-five-six.

KEY SIGNATURES

Together, sharps and flats are referred to as *accidentals*, and every key has its own set of accidentals, collectively called its *key signature*. The key signature is located at the beginning of a song, as well as at the beginning of each new line of music. The following key signature has three sharps:

When sharps or flats appear in a key signature, every time a note is written on that line or space, you don't have to indicate (with an accidental) that it's sharp or flat since the accidental already has been designated in the key signature. Consequently, key signatures make things easier to write. Of course, if there's a sharp in the key signature but you don't want the note to be sharped, you have to put a *natural* in front of the note. If you want the note sharped again in the same measure, you have to write out that sharp to counteract the previous natural:

In the subsequent measure, the key signature would apply again; therefore, you wouldn't need to write out the sharp again, though sometimes *courtesy accidentals* are provided.

Key Signatures with Flats

When flats occur in a key signature, they appear in the following order: B♭–E♭–A♭–D♭–G♭–C♭–F♭.

When your key signature contains flats and you're playing in a *major* key, a quick way to know what key you are in is to look at the second-to-last flat. *That* is the key! For instance, when you have four flats (B♭, E♭, A♭, and D♭), the second-to-last flat is A♭, so you are in the key of A♭ major:

A♭ major

When you have just one flat, you're in the key of F major:

F major

When your key signature contains flats and you're in a *minor* key, a quick way to know what key you're in is to count up two whole steps from the last flat. *That* is the key! For instance, when you have three flats, if you count up two whole steps from the last flat, A♭, you reach C. Thus, you're in the key of C minor:

C minor

If you have five flats, counting up two whole steps from the G♭, you reach B♭. You're in the key of B♭ minor:

B♭ minor

Key Signatures with Sharps

When sharps occur in a key signature, they appear in the following order: F♯–C♯–G♯–D♯–A♯–E♯–B♯. Notice how the order is exactly opposite of the order of the flats.

When your key signature contains sharps and you're playing in a *major* key, a quick way to know what key you are in is to look at the last sharp, then move up one half step. For instance, when you have two sharps (F♯ and C♯), move up one half step from C♯ to reach D, which is the key:

D major

When your key signature has sharps and you're in a *minor* key, a quick way to know what key you're in is to count down one whole step from the last sharp. For instance, when you have two sharps, count down one whole step from the last sharp, C♯, to reach B. You're in the key of B minor:

B minor

If you have four sharps, count down one whole step from the D♯ to reach C♯. You're in the key of C♯ minor:

C♯ minor

CHORD THEORY

You don't need to know theory to play music, but it can help you better understand the music that you play. If you'd like to learn more about the theory of chord construction, read on!

Triads

Triad is a Greek word that means "three," and that's exactly what a triad contains—three notes! Triads, the most common type of chord, are built by stacking two 3rds on top of each other. When we say "3rds," we're talking about *intervals*—the distance between notes. If you start on one note and move up the scale, the distance between the first note and the next note is a *2nd*. The distance between the first note and the third note is a *3rd*, between the first and fourth is a *4th*, and so on. Thirds can be either major or minor, and stacking these 3rds on top of each other in different combinations creates four types of triads: *major, minor, diminished*, and *augmented*. Here is a C major triad:

C major triad

root   3rd   5th

The defining note of a chord (its letter name) is called the *root*. Notice how the second note in the triad is the *3rd*. The top note is called the *5th* because its interval relative to the root is a 5th (count up yourself to see). After we take a closer look at intervals, we'll look at the different types of triads that you can build with those intervals.

Intervals

The *triad* section briefly defined an interval: the distance between any two notes. Counting up from the first note to the second note will give you the interval between those two notes, a *2nd*. That distance is quantified with a number, but intervals also have another component: their *quality*. The quality of any interval can be *major, minor, diminished, augmented*, or *perfect*. Looking at the 12 notes in a chromatic scale, along with their intervals, can help explain the differences between these qualities:

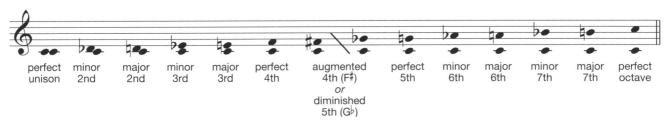

| perfect unison | minor 2nd | major 2nd | minor 3rd | major 3rd | perfect 4th | augmented 4th (F♯) *or* diminished 5th (G♭) | perfect 5th | minor 6th | major 6th | minor 7th | major 7th | perfect octave |

You may notice that every minor interval is one half step smaller than its major-interval counterpart. The only intervals that are not major or minor are the *perfect* intervals—the unison, 4th, 5th, and octave. Lowering a perfect interval (like the fifth) results in a *diminished* interval, while raising a perfect interval (like the fourth) results in an *augmented* interval. All of the other non-perfect intervals can be diminished or augmented as well, though it rarely happens. Here's how: If you lower a minor interval by one half step, it becomes diminished; if you raise a major interval by one half step, it becomes augmented.

Now let's look at all four types of triads that we can build with these intervals: *major, minor, diminished*, and *augmented*. Major triads have a major 3rd and a perfect 5th; minor triads have a minor 3rd and a perfect 5th; diminished triads have a minor 3rd and a diminished 5th; and augmented triads have a major 3rd and an augmented 5th:

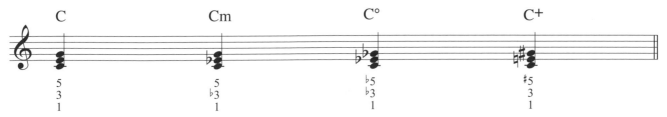

C	Cm	C°	C+
5	5	♭5	♯5
3	♭3	♭3	3
1	1	1	1

Major triads are labeled with just a letter (for example, C), minor triads are labeled with a lowercase "m" (Cm), diminished triads are labeled with a "°" (C°), and augmented triads are labeled with a "+" (C+).

Seventh Chords

Seventh chords are four-note chords that add the interval of a 7th above the root of a triad. Five types of unaltered 7th chords exist: *dominant 7th* (labeled with a "7" after the chord's letter name), *minor seventh* (m7), *major seventh* (maj7), *minor-major 7th* (m[maj7]), and *half-diminished 7th* (ø7). The 7th chords (with C as the root) are illustrated below:

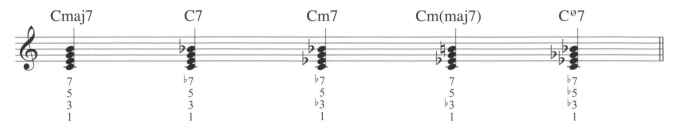

Extended Chords

Beyond 7th chords, you can add further extensions to color the chord even more. Basically, you continue stacking 3rds on top of a 7th chord to build extended chords. Stack one 3rd on top and you have a 9th chord; add a 3rd to the 9th chord and you have an 11th chord; and add a 3rd to that 11th chord to get a 13th chord.

Not all notes of an extended chord are necessary to complete the chord. This is especially true on guitar, where a full 13th chord would be impossible to play, since you'd need to play seven notes but only have six strings! However, some of the notes are more important to include than others. For a chord to be an extended chord, you have to include the 7th and the extension. After that, including the 3rd, root, and other extensions holds lesser priority. The least important note to include in an extended chord is the 5th.

It's also important to note that extensions can appear in a different octave than their numerical name implies. For instance, a 13th played down one octave is a 6th. You can use that 6th (instead of a 13th) in your chord, and, as long as the 7th is present, it will still be considered a 13th chord.

Suspended, "Add," and Other Chords

Suspended ("sus") chords are formed when a note is substituted for a chord tone. In a sus4 chord, for instance, the 4th is substituted for the 3rd. "Add" chords are simply chords that add one or several notes to any particular chord. The difference between a sus4 and an add4 chord is that the sus4 does not include the 3rd, while the add4 does. Of course a few exceptions exist. A triad with an added 6th is simply referred to as a 6th chord (though it could be written as an add6 chord), and a chord with the 6th and the 9th added is simply called a "six-nine" chord.

Altered Chords

Any chord can be altered, and that alteration is reflected in the chord's name. For instance, if you alter a 7th chord by lowering the 5th one half step, you have a 7♭5 chord; raise the 5th of that 7th chord by one half step, and you have a 7♯5 chord.

Inversions

Any time that the lowest sounding note in a chord is not the root, the chord is in *inversion*. The more notes you have in a chord, the more possible inversions you have. For instance, a 7th chord can be played in more inversions than a triad.

Same Shapes, Different Names

Many chords can be called more than one name. For instance, a ♭5th is equivalent to a ♯11, and a chord containing one of these notes could be labeled either way. Likewise, a ♯5th and a ♭13th are also equivalent.